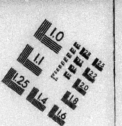

IMAGE EVALUATION
TEST TARGET (MT-3)

Photographic
Sciences
Corporation

23 WEST MAIN STREET
WEBSTER, N.Y. 14580
(716) 872-4503

CIHM/ICMH
Microfiche
Series.

CIHM/ICMH
Collection de
microfiches.

Canadian Institute for Historical Microreproductions / Institut canadien de microreproductions historiques

1	2	3

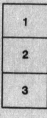

1	2	3
4	5	6

CHARGES

TO BE

DELIVERED

AT THE

INITIATION OF MEMBERS

TO THE

SEVERAL ORDERS

OF THE

Loyal Orange Association:

TO WHICH ARE ADDED

SERVICES

FOR THE

BURIAL OF ORANGEMEN,

THE

DEDICATION OF AN ORANGE LODGE,

AND FOR THE

INSTALLATION OF OFFICERS.

TORONTO:

BRO. J. CLELAND, PRINTER, 62 YONGE STREET.

1856.

Samuel H Babcock

ORANGE ORDER.

A CHARGE

To be Delivered to the Brethren after the Ceremonies and Pass-words are given in the Orange.

BROTHER,

The Mysteries and Secrets connected with the Orange Institution have now been communicated to you, and if you will observe them, and conform to the Obligation you have freely and voluntarily assumed, we shall have cause to rejoice in the steps we have taken to Initiate you; but should you fail to observe them, then will our sorrow be great; firstly, on account of your fall, and secondly, on account of the injury that will thereby be done to our Institution.

I entreat you, let your Obligation be your guide! Should the perpetration of crime ever enter your mind, reflect upon what you have now sworn—and let it be a check to every evil thought that human weakness may suggest.

I have further to admonish you against the snares that may be laid for you by our enemies, and to impress upon your mind the great value of *caution*—so that you weigh well every expression you may use in connection with the Order. Be ever watchful when the Order is at work, so that you may gain wisdom by listening to the advice and opinion of your seniors; and when you have heard, may you be wise to reflect, and speak not—and that you treasure up the lessons in your heart, to the end that you may prove your great faith. There are two cardinal virtues which bind the Brotherhood of our Order—they are *Union* and *Truth*. By the honorable

exercise of the latter, in all your intercourse with the world,
and especially with the Brotherhood, you will find that the
former is to be and will be maintained. Regard them then
as the apple of your eye, only to be parted with in death.

I trust what I have said to you in the name of the Lodge
will have its due weight; and now, allow me to introduce
you to those, whom you are hereafter to regard as Brethren.

My Brethren, receive this Brother to your friendship and
love.

[If more than one Candidate be introduced the Charge is
to be reserved until all are initiated.]

PURPLE ORDER.

A CHARGE

*To be Delivered to the Brethren after the Ceremonies and
Pass-words are given in the Royal Purple.*

BROTHER,

You have now received the Second Degree of
our Order—and you may regard it as an addition to your character and standing, for none are advanced but the faithful;
none pass the fiery ordeal of the burning furnace, but such as
have well and faithfully served in the probationary degree. I
therefore congratulate you upon your avancement. We have
not judged you from appearance—but we have narrowly
watched your conduct, and the result is, you have been held
worthy of the degree now conferred.

The Order itself will afford you ample scope for consideration and reflection; it will also materially assist your understanding, and render you a more efficient and worthy member.
On a former occasion you were told what were your duties,
and what the Brethren would expect from you; those duties

are now the more binding, as you stand higher in the Order.
You must at all times see, that the Rules and Regulations of
the Order, and the mandates and Decrees of the Grand Lodge
are strictly obeyed and enforced. You are not to conceal the
faults of a Brother from the Brotherhood—but you are, as far
as possible, to screen him from the censure of the world, and
to do all that is in your power for his reformation. You are
at all times to treat his foibles with candour, and to admonish
in friendship.

Having thus secured to yourself this advancement, it is
hoped that by your continued practice of all that is good and
commendable, and your avoidance of all that is bad and cen-
surable, you will not give us cause to regret the step we have
taken in advancing you as we have now done.

BLUE ORDER.

A CHARGE

*To be Delivered to the Brethren after the Ceremonies and
Pass-words are given in the Royal Blue.*

BROTHER,
    I congratulate you upon your admission to this
Degree, because it is the first which calls upon you for the
exercise of greater activity and a nobler zeal. It is to prove
to you a beacon of light; it is to exhibit to you a lesson for
curbing your most anxious desires, and to keep your passions
and prejudices under proper subjection.

The bearing of this Degree is to bring your mind to the
consideration of eternity. It is to prove to you, by the Star
in the East, that arrested its course over Bethlehem, how
small beginnings can, by the decree of an all-wise Providence, have great and glorious terminations. It is to teach
you the duty of being satisfied with your lot, when you re-

member your Saviour's nativity and his high destination. Reflect that, however humble your position, by a constant life of virtue and faith, you may arrive at as near a state of perfection as sinful man can expect to attain.

It now becomes your duty, narrowly to watch your Brethren of the inferior Degrees. You are mildly to correct their errors, and to remonstrate with them upon their approach to any evil action, and thus prove to them the worth and value of your exalted station. You must at all times exert yourself to keep our glorious Institution from harm, and not allow the precincts of the Star to be desecrated. By your submission to your seniors, you will convince your inferiors of their duty to do likewise. Although you are particularly to see the sufferings and the wants of your Brethren relieved, yet by virtue of that brilliant guide, which you have this day pursued, you must feel that your benevolence should be universal. And lastly, you are to observe, with scrupulous exactitude, the secrecy of the degree just conferred; and you are to absent yourself from any Lodge that does not faithfully carry out the principles we teach. By doing which you will prove that our confidence in you has not been misplaced.

ROYAL ARCH ORDER.

CHARGE
To be delivered after the Initiation in the Royal Arch.

BROTHER,

You have been now admitted, after strict trial, to this exalted Degree. It must have proved to you many facts, which, if duly thought of, may tend to inform your mind, and to render less obdurate the propensity inherent in man, to sin. Reflect, and you will see, that man is not regarded by Orangemen on account of his worldly wealth; it is the wealth of the soul that we prize, not that which, when we perish can avail nothing. Reflect, and you will have good cause to remember how much it has become your duty to render assistance to a Brother in distress. Reflect, and you will find that much of your duty is enforced upon you by implication, which a clear mind, seeking for justice, will at once discover.

Remember, then, your duty and your obligations; and also how fatal and dark will be your plunge, from this to eternal death, should you neglect them. Remember, also, that it is only by obedience to the Great Father in Heaven, you can expect to pass from the darkness of this world to the light of everlasting life, and that prayer, and the practice of all that is good, together with a strong reliance upon your Saviour, can alone lead to this. Remember, too, that you prayed as being under the canopy of Heaven, therefore take heed and recall to your mind the solemn hour of death, the awful one of judgment, and, lastly, eternity.

A lesson has been taught you, how these may be overcome; and if you hope to gain eternal life, I warn you that it is essential that you have faith; for no one can, in his weakness and sinfulness, expect to be perfect. If therefore, you hope for the charitable aid and intercession of our Saviour, do you extend *Charity* to others.

In every way you are taught to avoid sin. Even when least expected, the serpent may be in your path. I therefore entreat you, as you hope for salvation hereafter, that you do not omit any occasion, in which you may find opportunities to fulfil the vows you have now made.

ROYAL SCARLET ORDER.

CHARGE

To be Delivered to a Royal Scarlet Companion.

COMPANION,

Having passed through the various Degrees of the Brotherhood, you have at last been admitted to Companionship in this Illustrious Chapter. You will have observed, through every grade that the Word of GOD is the Brilliant Star which is to be your guide through life. It is expected of you that you will not treat life lightly; and that you are to hold it as in trust from your Heavenly Father, to be employed in acts of faith and charity; and we trust that whenever you shall be called upon, you will draw and wield your sword in defence of our glorious Institution and the Protestant faith. After the obligation you have taken, it will only be requisite to remind you, that you will at all times be called upon to conform to the ceremonies, rules, and regulations of the Chapter. Prove yourself, my friend and Companion, my Brother and fellow-labourer, to be a child of humility, charity, and hospitality, and we shall never regret the promotion we have now given you. For remember, my Brother and Companion, that this Order of Royal Scarlet, is to be regarded by all as the safeguard of our Institution, and can never be violated; for its doors will ever be closed against those who have, in the remotest manner possible, brought corruption into any order that preceded it. As a Companion of the Royal Scarlet, you, with those who have preceded you in this Chapter, are bound to give alms to the poor and weary pilgrim, travelling from afar, to succour the needy, feed the hungry, clothe the naked, and bind up the wounds of the afflicted. We are to be lovers of peace; but we are bound to war against the enemies of innocence, destitute widows, helpless orphans, and the Protestant faith; and may the Almighty, who is a strong tower of strength and defence to all those who put their trust in him, be your support and your salvation.

FUNERAL SERVICE.

"Bury the dead" is the first of charitable duties, and if this mandate is compulsory, generally speaking, how much more ought it to be observed in particular, by the members of a Protestant Association. It is an occasion on which we are allowed to forget past errors, and to think only of the good which our friend or brother has done. We are allowed to review, on such occasions, the relations between the living and the dead, and to draw from the past admonitions for the future.

In as much as we are a Protestant body, and as the service which is here laid down may not suit the desires or wishes of all, it should be well remembered, that neither these nor any other formalities should be used by the Brotherhood, unless by the special request of the deceased, while living; which desire should at all times be communicated to the senior officer of the Lodge to which he belonged. Taking it for granted that these preliminaries have been complied with, the following is the order to be observed:—

The Lodge must be summoned. If more than the members of the Lodge of which deceased died a member attend, no seniority of office, save that of a Grand Officer, shall be claimed. The senior Officer present of the Lodge of which the deceased died a member shall preside; but in case the Brother deceased was member of a distant Lodge, then the Master of the senior Lodge present shall preside.

The Lodge is then opened in due form.

The Roll is called, and when the name of the deceased Brother is announced—

DEPUTY MASTER.—Worshipful Master and Brethren, it hath pleased Almighty God to terminate the existence of our Brother on earth. Is it meet and proper that we mourn for him?

MASTER.—It is meet and proper that we should mourn for our departed Brother, and that we accompany his mortal remains to its last home. (Here the Master affixes a crape tied around on his left arm, and the brethren do likewise.)

MASTER.—Brother Secretary, what Degrees did our deceased Brother enjoy?

[SECRETARY.—Here announces the Degrees.]

MASTER.—Let each Brother be furnished with a Rosette, to be used as required.

[The Rozettee to be made of Orange and the highest Degree obtained.]

This being done, the Master shall appoint Bearers. The Lodge shall then form in Procession, and proceed to the house where the dead Brother lies.

Nothing is then done, except accompanying the corpse to the grave. The burial service having taken place, the Master at the head of the grave, the Secretary by his side with the Roll, the following shall be the service, which is to be considered additional, and not as superceding any portion of the services established, and performed by Ministers of the Gospel.

MASTER.—Brethren—In the death of this our departed Brother, we have another record of the uncertainty of life, and the vanity of human labour and pursuits, if sought merely for our own glory. He knoweth no more our love; yet while we mourn for the absence of our Brother, while we pray and hope that his immortal soul may be in Elysium, let us not forget our own mortality and weakness; but let us reflect, that as this our departed Brother now is, so shall we soon be.

Death is of frequent occurrence; and yet, my Brethren, we do not find that our thoughts are more given to it. But one moment's reflection, and we remember that the Lord giveth and the Lord taketh away. We know that he hath given us life; and we know that this gift must, and will terminate. From day to day, we proceed, thinking only of the end of our projects, but never reflecting that death may come upon us like the thief in the night, to end our career before our projects are fulfilled. Let death come upon us when it will, we are unprepared.

Let us remember, my Brethren, that we now look upon the grave of a friend—that instead of his body, we behold even now before us, the narrow habitation in which we have delivered dust to dust, and that all are levelled by it; let us then make ourselves useful while life remains; let us as Brethren of a great Brotherhood, implicitly follow the Christian doctrines of our Order, and thus be prepared as far as possible to do our work of faith; let us not only by our words, but let our practice show it forth in our lives. In this manner, my friends and Brethren, we may meet our God and our Redeemer with hope.

As it is no portion of our duty to our late Brother to eulogise him beyond his deserts, so shall it be our duty to draw a veil over his foibles, and to bury them with him. We know, that however good and righteous a man may be, there is not that being upon earth who doeth good, and sinneth not; and while we deplore the weakness of our nature, let us at the same time with unswerving integrity follow out and inculcate the doctrines of our Order.

MASTER.—(The right hand elevated.) Brethren, our Brother is dead!

BRETHREN.—Not to us.

MASTER.—Brethren, his name has passed from us.

BRETHREN.—We will inscribe it in our memories, and our works shall yet exhibit it.

MASTER.—Let Israel hope in the Lord, from henceforth and for ever.

PRAYER.

Lord God of Righteousness, depending on thy mercy, and on thy power and on thy promises declared unto mankind, we now humbly beseech Thee hear our prayers which we offer at the Throne of thy Eternal Kingdom: Save this Brotherhood from the pains of eternal death, and bring them to everlasting life. Direct us in our last hours, and bring us safely to thy glory, there to reunite, for the sake of our Lord and Saviour.

Here in solemn silence the Master, then all the Brethren,

drop the Rosettes into the grave, and the Brethren standing immediately around the grave shall then throw in a handfull, or a shovelfull of earth on the coffin. The grave being carefully filled up, the Secretary shall take the number of the grave post, or any other symbol by which graves are traced, and shall, on his return to the Lodge, record it in the book with the particulars of the Funeral.

CEREMONY
For Dedicating a Hall or Lodge Room.

When the Officers and Members of the Lodge meet, let a Master of Ceremonies be appointed, to introduce visitors, who, as they arrive, are to be conducted to their seats. This having been accomplished, and the hour for receiving visitors having elapsed, the Officers of the Lodge shall retire to Robe, all the Members, except the Master of Ceremonies, following.

The Officers being Robed, shall enter the Room, and take their seats; it being understood, that in entering they are to be preceded by an armed Tyler, and followed by another, the last, seeing the officers in their places, shall retire outside of the Lodge Room. Then shall the inner Tyler advance to the front of the Master, who shall say:

Master.—On your peril, Brother, allow no one Ingress or Egress into or from this Hall, who gives not the pass. The Tyler returns to the door.

[The special Pass of the Day is given to the Deputy Master, to whom, those wishing to obtain it must apply.]

Then the Members of the Orange Order, each decorated with an Orange Sash, preceded by their own Tyler, to be appointed for the occasion, having been announced, and having obtained permission from the Master to enter, shall enter, two and two, and take their seats, the Tyler with a Wand of the Order, standing, saying to the Master,—

"Worshipful, the Brethren of the Orange are present."

Then the announcement shall be made to the Master in the words following.

Tyler at the Door within.—Worshipful, the Brethren of the Royal Purple are in attendance.

Master.—Admit the Royal Purple Brethren.

Then the Purplemen, all decorated with the order, preceded by their Tyler, shall enter, and being conducted to their Station, their Tyler shall say:

"Worshipful, the Brethren of the Royal Purple are present." He remains standing.

Then the following announcement from

The *Inward Tyler.*—"The Brethren of the Royal Blue attend."

Master.—Admit the Brethren of the Royal Blue.

Then the Brethren of the Blue, all decorated with the Order, preceded by their Tyler, shall enter, and being in their seats, the Tyler shall say:

"Worshipful, the Brethren of the Royal Blue are present."

Then the following announcement shall be made, the Tyler advancing three steps to the Master:

"Worshipful, the Brethren of the Royal Arch attend."

Master.—Tylers, to your Stations.

Then the Tylers of the three Orders present, together with the inner Tyler, shall form an Arch with their staves, wide enough for the Royal Arch Brethren to pass under, two abreast.

Master.—Admit our Brethren of the Royal Arch Purple Mark.

As soon as this announcement is made, the Members of the three Orders present shall rise, and remain standing until the Brethren of he Royal Arch are seated. The Brethren of the Royal Arch are not accompanyed by a Tyler, their Tyler is at the door within.

An announcement is now made by the sound of a trumpet without.

Master.—Tyler of the Royal Arch, go to the Portico, and see who is at the gate of our temple.

Tyler making his obeisance, retires.

Master.—Tyler, of the Royal Arch, what Report?

Tyler.—A Herald, announcing the approach of Illustrious Knight's Companions, Brethren come to grace and honour our ceremonies.

Master Rising.—Brethren and friends, we will receive these Illustrious Companions. Brethren of the Arch, Brethren of the Blue, Brethren of the Purple, and Brethren of the Orange, send forth two of your Senior Members.

The Senior Members then come forth and stand in front of the Master.

Master.—Brethren, proceed to the audience Chamber, there receive the Illustrious Knights, and conduct them hither.

The Senior Brethren then retire.

Master.—Tyler of the Royal Arch, admit the Illustrious Companions of the Scarlet, when they approach without further ceremony.

A Pause.

The blast of a Trumpet.

Enter.   Two   and   two

The Orangemen,—the Purplemen,

The Blue,—the Royal Arch.

Herald of the day.

Companions of the Scarlet, two and two.

A Companion with a Cushion suspended in front

of him, upon which is

A Bible open,

A Crown,

A Sword.

The Sovereign, or Representative and Chaplain,

Herald.

Being all in the Room, a halt is made, the Companions and Brethren, all but the Brother who bears the Bible, divide in open column, the Brother bearing the Bible then advances, and takes his seat on the left of the Master; the Sovereign, or his Representative and Chaplain then advance.

The Master shall then conduct the Grand Officer present to his seat, the Chaplain going to the seat on the right of the

Throne, and the Master, takes the place assigned to him in the Ceremonies.

All being seated, the Master of the Lodge, rising, shall say :—

"Right Worshipful, it is the wish of the Brethren of this Lodge, number ——, of Loyal Orangemen, to have this their Edifice, dedicated to the Almighty and the cause of Protestantism."

G. M.—Let their wishes and good intentious be consummated. Let us now commence our exercises Brethren, let us sing.

Then shall be sung PSALM XXIX.

> Ye princes that in might excel,
>   Your grateful sacrifice prepare,
> God's glorious actions loudly tell,
>   His wondrous pow'r to all declare.
> To His great name fresh altars raise,
>   Devoutly, due respect afford ;
> Him in His holy temple praise,
>   Where He's with solemn state adored.
> When God in thunder loudly speaks,
>   And scattered flames of lightning sends,
> The forest nods, the desert quakes,
>   And stubborn Kadish lowly bends.
> God rules the angry floods on high,
>   His boundless sway shall never cease,
> His saints with strength he will supply,
>   And bless his own with constant peace.

Grand Chaplain.—Brethren, let us pray.

To Thee, O God, the worker of all signs, to whom all praise is due, we now bend in humble supplication. Thy name, O Lord, will we exalt, and our hearts shall confess thine excellence and holiness. Thee, O Lord, do we thank, in that thou hast vouchsafed unto us strength and wisdom to erect and dedicate this Edifice to the glory of Thy revealed will, through our Lord and Saviour. Teach us, O Lord, on this day of rejoicing, to invoke thy glory, and send down upon this our humble sanctuary, the power and splendour of thine all-gracious protection. For thine unbounded kindness to us and to our cause, O Thou, our living God,—for thy great and all-sufficient aid, in bringing thy Church and people through their fiery ordeals, receive our humble thanks. We praise Thee, O Lord, that Thou hast redeemed thy people from the thraldom of Popery, and we magnify thy name, that Thou hast given them strength to withstand the assaults of the enemy. Lord, hear our prayers, now and evermore, for Christ's sake! Amen.

The Brethren rise, and while standing the G. Master shall say:

" In the name of the Father, the Son and the Holy Ghost."

The Master of the Lodge shall then light one of the Lodge Candles, and place it in front of the Ark.

"I now solemnly dedicate this Hall to the Almighty Father in Heaven, and to the Protestant cause."

The Deputy Master shall now light another of the Lodge Candles, and place it also near the Ark.

" Now and for evermore !"—Amen.

The Senior Committee–man shall now light the third candle and place it also near the Ark. Then the Master, Deputy Master, and Senior Committee-man, shall each take one of the lights, and arrange them in their places. The Ark shall then be taken by them, and preceded by the Officers of the Lodge, shall be carried three times round the room, the G.C. saying,

"And they departed from the mount of the Lord, three days' journey; and the Ark of the Covenant of the Lord went before them in three days' journey, to search out a resting place for them. And the Cloud of the Lord was before them by day, when they went out of the Camp. And it came to pass, when the Ark set forward, that Moses said, Rise up, Lord, and let thine enemies be scattered, and let them that hate thee flee before Thee."

[Here set the Ark down in the centre of the Room.]

"And when it rested, he said, Return O Lord, unto the many thousands of Israel."—NUMBERS x. 33, 34, 35, & 36.

All being seated, the Grand Master shall say :

"Blessed and extolled be the Lord our God; whose gracious providence has been so kindly extended to the Protestant Church. He is the helper of those who seek Him, and the comforter of those who trust in Him. Blessed at all times be His Holy name.

In the Dedication of this Edifice to the Almighty, we but offer up a faint expression of our hopes and desires· Far from us be the thought of exalting ourselves by this act of humility; but may we ever, with the same eagerness and devotedness, offer up our lives and our fortunes, to preserve and maintain the principles of this glorious Institution. Let us supplicate our Almighty Father, through the mediation of his beloved Son, that he will never fail us in our distress. Let us supplicate for His merciful aid, to avert all danger from the Throne of our Protestant Sovereign. Let us pray that the principles which led our fathers to the great and glorious revolution to put down Popery, may never abate, but that they may be perpetuated with never-fading glory to the end of time.

Grand Chaplain.—Now, O Lord, we beseech thee that thou wilt bless us as thou hast promised, when we gather together in thy name. Bless this our undertaking, and grant that we may prosper in our New Edifice. Endue us, O Lord, with understanding, to comprehend and fulfil thy word and will. We beseech Thee by the dream of *Jacob*,—we implore thee by the meekness of *Moses*, comfort us, as thou didst Joshua, when from morning till eventide, he fought against the enemies of thy people. Let the morning Star be to us, as the bright harbinger that led the way for the wise men of the East, and arrested their progress, when thou alone wert present.

All being seated, the Grand Master shall say:
Brother Worshipful, bring forth the word of God.

The Master shall then take the Bible, and bearing it open, shall walk round the Lodge and the Ark, the Grand Master saying:

And it came to pass when Moses had made an end of writing the words of this Law in a Book, until they were finished, that Moses commanded the Levites which bare the Ark of the Covenant of the Lord, saying, take this Book of the Law, and put it in the side of the Ark of the Covenant of the Lord your God, that it may be for a witness against ye.

(Here the Bible is deposited.)

NOW LET US SING.

Sound the loud timbrel o'er Egypt's dark sea;
Jehovah has triumphed, his people are free.
Sing, for the pride of the tyrant is broken;
    His chariots, his horsemen, all splendid and brave;
How vain was their boasting, the Lord hath but spoken,
    And chariots and horsemen are sunk in the wave;
Sound the loud timbrel o'er Egypt's dark sea;
Jehovah has triumphed, his people are free.
Praise to the Conqueror; praise to the Lord;
His word was our arrow, his breath was our sword.
Who shall return to tell Egypt the story
Of those she sent forth in the hour of her pride?
The Lord hath looked out from his pillar of glory,
And all her brave thousands are dash'd in the tide.
Praise to the Conqueror; praise to the Lord;
    His word was our arrow, his breath was our sword.

(Here the Addresses if any.)

(Grand Chaplain shall read the following verses.)

19. Have respect therefore to the prayer of thy servant and to his supplication, O Lord my God, to hearken unto the cry and the prayer which thy servant prayeth before thee:

20. That thine eyes may be open upon this house day and night, upon the place whereof thou hast said that thou wouldest put thy name there; to hearken unto the prayer which thy servant prayeth toward this place.

21. Hearken therefore unto the supplications of thy servant, and of thy people Israel, which they shall make toward this place: hear thou from thy dwelling place, even from heaven; and when thou hearest, forgive.

34. If thy people go out to war against their enemies by the way that thou shalt send them, and they pray unto thee toward this city which thou hast chosen, and the house which I have built for thy name;

35. Then hear thou from the heavens their prayer and their supplication, and maintain their cause.

Then sing "God Save the Queen,"

God save our gracious Queen,
Long live our noble Queen,
   God save the Queen!
Send her victorious,
Happy and glorious,
Long to reign over us,
   God save the Queen!

O Lord our God! arise,
Scatter her enemies,
   And make them fall!
Confound their politics,
Frustrate their popish tricks,
On her our hearts we fix,—
   God save us all!

The Grand Chaplain shall then close with the Lord's Prayer:—

THE LORD'S PRAYER.

"Our Father which art in Heaven, Hallowed be thy name. Thy kingdom come. Thy will be done on earth, as it is in heaven. Give us this day our daily bread. And forgive us our trespasses as we forgive them that trespass against us. And lead us not into temptation, but deliver us from evil; for thine is the kingdom, and the power and the glory, for ever. Amen.

FORM OF
INSTALLATION OF OFFICERS.

The Lodge shall be opened as usual. The Master Elect, to take his Seat on the left of the Secretary, and before proceeding with any other business put the test to know if all have the annual.

AFTER THE LODGE IS OPENED.

D. M.—Brother past Secretary upon whom has the choice of this Worshipful Lodge fallen, to be the Master for the current year.

Bro. Sec'y.—Having confidence in the Worshipful Brother ———, and having had frequent proofs of his ability and desire to advance the cause of our glorious Institution, we have selected him for our Master and now require his installation. I now present to you Brother ———.

D. M. or Chaplain.—Let us pray, (all kneel) Master and Creator of the World, disposer of life and death, we entreat thee look down upon us with mercy and bless our undertaking! We humbly crave, that thou wilt at all times give us wisdom to govern our actions and judgment to guide and govern the actions of those under our care; endue us with a desire to conduct all our undertakings, in peace, brotherly love and kindness. Permit the Master of this Lodge to enjoy the grace, and give him the light of Wisdom, so that he may impart it to those, whose conduct he may be called upon to scrutinize. May Faith, Hope and Charity, Justice, Temperance, Prudence and Fortitude, ever be his guide and the guide of us all, for Christ's sake.

Lodge.—Amen.

D. M.—Brother ——— before you are sworn into office, let me ask of you, if you are prepared to act under the Constitution and laws of the Loyal Orange Institution ?

M.—I am.

D. M.—By your consent you take upon yourself various

duties, not only will you be required to follow them yourself, which from the fact, of your being chosen to the station you are to occupy, is proof you will, but you assume the office of Guardian and Adviser to the Members of your Lodge. You will rebuke them for a violation of any portion of their obligations, as a superior Brother should rebuke an inferior. You are required to warn them, that it is their duty to live peaceably with, and act honourably towards all men, and especially towards a brother; and that they are bound strictly to guard against all unworthy excesses. You will teach them to denounce an impostor, and to cherish the faithful amongst our Brethren.

Master Elect.—I acknowledge these obligations to be my duty, and will endeavour, with the help of God, to discharge them.

(Then administer the Oath, Members all standing.)

OBLIGATION OF A MASTER AND DEPUTY MASTER.

I, A. B., swear, that I do not undertake the office of Master for any private or personal emolument or advantage; that I will use the authority with which I may be invested as Master, to keep proper behavior and sobriety in the Lodge, over which I am to preside, and to cause a due observance of the rules and regulations of the Society, by all the Members of my Lodge; and lastly, I swear, that I will not certify for any person, without having first proved him, and being satisfied in my conscience, that he is a person of good character.

OBLIGATION OF A SECRETARY.

I, A. B., do swear, that I will faithfully preserve the books, papers and all other documents of the Lodge, that may be committed to my charge; that I will not myself sign, or seal, or cause to be signed, or sealed, nor part with the Lodge seal, so that it may be affixed to any forged paper, or irregular Orangeman's Certificate; and lastly, that I will deliver up all the property of the Lodge when requested by the Master or other competent authorities so to do.

OBLIGATION OF A TREASURER.

I, A. B., do swear, that I will faithfully preserve all the monies or other property, that I may receive for the use of my Lodge, and that I will fairly account for the same, when requested so to do by the Master and officers of the Lodge.

OBLIGATION OF A COMMITTEE-MAN.

I, A. B., do solemnly swear, that I will exercise the privileges, functions, and duties of a Committee-man, faithfully, conscientiously, and impartially; that I will use whatever influence I may possess for the benefit of my Lodge particularly; and generally for the interest of the Order, to the best of my skill, knowledge, and cunning.

(The Master then takes his Seat, and the other officers are obligated.)

Deputy Master.
Treasurer.
Secretary.
Senior Committee-man, and the Members of the Committee. The Master saying to each as he swears them in.

Master.—You have heard the duties which I have assumed, for the sake of this Lodge. The like duties' must you assume before you can be duly installed. Do you consent, as I have done, that these Virtues and Obligations shall be your guide.

Deputy Master.—I do.

(Then administer the Oath.)
(Repeat the same form for the other officers.)
(The Committee may be all sworn together.)

Chaplain.—Father of mercies, look down upon us, with grace, and unite us still closer in the bond of union, by which we are united as one family, give us wisdom to know thy ways, and a heart to love one another, for our Saviour's sake. "Behold, how good and how pleasant it is for brethren to dwell together in unity! It is like the precious ointment upon the beard, even Aaron's beard; that went down to the skirts of his garment; as the dew of Hermon, and as the dew that descended upon the mountains of Zion; for there the Lord commanded the blessing, even life for evermore."—*Psalm,* 133.

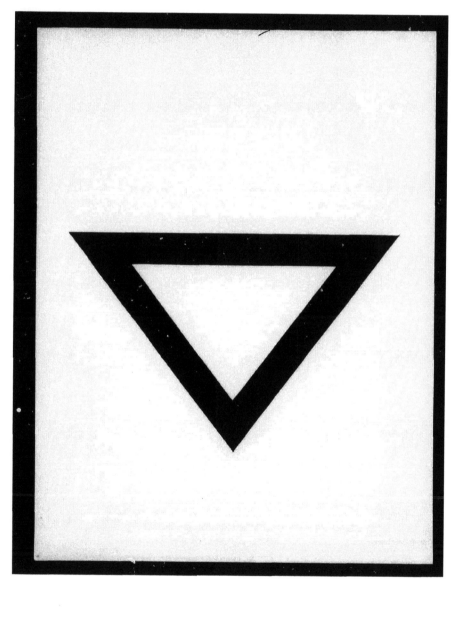

Lightning Source UK Ltd.
Milton Keynes UK
UKHW020626070222
398308UK00005B/251